MENSA
LATERAL THINKING

THIS IS A CARLTON BOOK

This edition produced for Book Sales Inc.

Text and puzzle content copyright © British Mensa Limited 1998
Design and artwork copyright © Carlton Books Limited 1998

All rights reserved.

This book is sold subject to the conditions that it shall not, by way of trade or otherwise, be lent, resold, hired out or otherwise circulated without the publisher's prior written consent in any form of cover or binding other than that in which it is published and without a similar condition including this condition, being imposed upon the subsequent purchaser.

ISBN 0-7858-0956-2

Layout: Adam Wright
Illustrations: Tim Sell

Printed and bound in Italy

MENSA® LATERAL THINKING

Dave Chatten and Carolyn Skitt

AMERICAN MENSA LTD

American Mensa Ltd is an organization for individuals who have one common trait: an IQ in the top 2% in the nation. Over 50,000 current members have found out how smart they are. This leaves room for an additional 4.5 million members in America alone. You may be one of them.

Looking for intellectual stimulation?

If you enjoy mental exercise, you'll find lots of good "workout programs" in the *Mensa Bulletin*, our national magazine. Voice your opinion in one of the newsletters published by each of our 150 local chapters. Learn from the many books and publications that are available to you as a member.

Looking for social interaction?

Are you a "people person," or would you like to meet other people with whom you feel comfortable? Then come to our local meetings, parties, and get-togethers. Participate in our lectures and debates. Attend our regional events and national gatherings. There's something happening on the Mensa calendar almost daily. So, you have lots of opportunities to meet people, exchange ideas, and make interesting new friends.

Looking for others who share your special interest?

Whether yours is as common as crossword puzzles or as esoteric as Egyptology, there's a Mensa Special Interest Group (SIG) for it.

Take the challenge. Find out how smart you really are. Mensans love to read so already have something in common.

Contact American Mensa Ltd today and ask for a free brochure. We enjoy adding new members and ideas to our high-IQ organization.

American Mensa Ltd
201 Main Street, Suite 1101
Fort Worth, Texas 76102

or, if you don't live in the USA:

Mensa International
15 The Ivories
628 Northampton Street
London N1 2NY
England   will be happy to put you in touch with your own national Mensa

CONTENTS

How to Join Mensa 4

Lateral Thinking Puzzles 7

Answers 123

The Mountaineers

A family of 4 were going on a mountaineering holiday. The second morning they were all found dead in their cabin. The coroner declared that they had all died from drowning. The faucets in the cabin had not been left on and the boiler and water storage units were undamaged. There was no sign of any foul play. What caused them to drown?

Clues
1. They were a mile from the nearest lake.
2. It had not rained for 5 days. Not a flash flood.
3. It was not caused by problems with a dam.

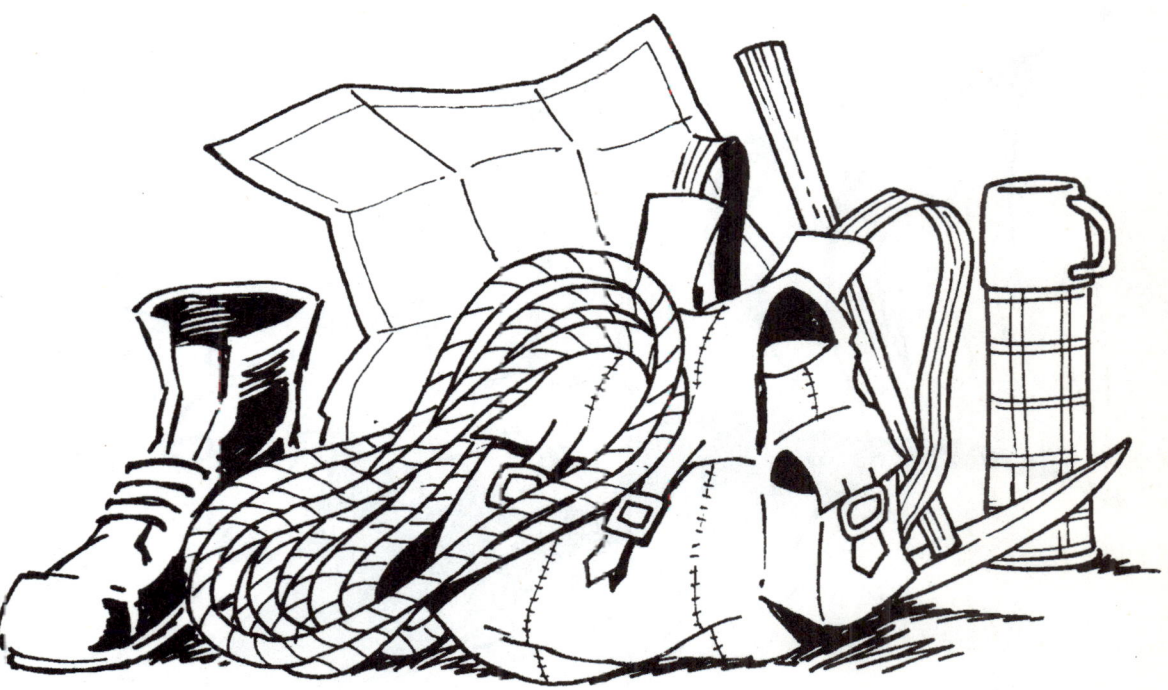

See answer 116

Arise

A man was exploring a mountain when he slipped and fell. He was 150ft from the summit when he slipped, but he was at the top after the slip. He did not climb the rest of the way and he was not lifted to the top by colleagues. How did he slip to the top?

Clues

1. He was on the same mountain and the top was above him.
2. He was not supported by a balloon filled with hydrogen or helium.
3. No ropes or pulleys were involved.
4. No thermals were involved.

See answer 68

High Days and Holidays

King Henry wanted to change all of the high days and holidays and called his ministers together. He decreed that holidays would occur on the high day and on the low day of each week, and these were Saturday and Friday respectively. If his week was in the order of high days going downwards to the low day, what would the sequence be?

See answer 38

The Share-Out

Three children were counting the money that they had when they found that they each had only one value of coin. Each child had a different value of coin and each had different numbers of coins. They calculated that if each child gave two of their coins to each of the other two children, they would all have the same amount of money.

If they finished with $1.80 each, how many of each coin did each child have to start with?

See answer 103

My Homework is Right!

At a local infant school a teacher gave the children a few math problems for homework. The next day the teacher pulled Tom out and told him that he had all of his wrong.
His answers to the problems set were:

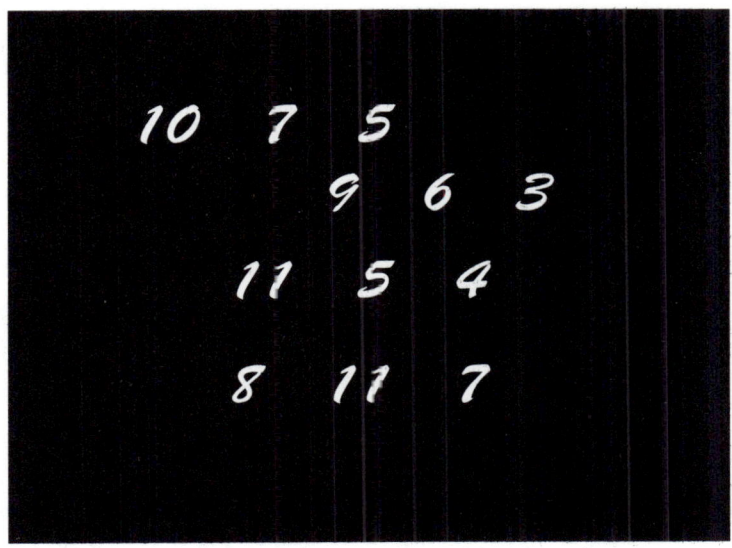

Tom was also right. How was this so?

See answer 90

Bob the Miser's Last Will

Old Bob was a miserly man who never spent his money. His 'Last Will and Testament' stated that he wished to be cremated together with the proceeds of his estate. He did not wish to give his money to his relatives.

When the will was read, the relatives stated that Bob was not sane when he made the will. The judge ruled that he was and Bob's wishes should be followed.

The Judge did, however, find a way to comply with Bob's wishes and at the same time please the relatives. How was this done?

See answer 109

A-Haunting We Will Go!

An ancient castle had been converted into a hotel. After a few months, many ghostly sightings had been reported. The manager was under pressure as many bookings were being lost, but he was getting some business from ghost hunters. The problem was that he could not guarantee to match the appearances with the right guests, until one day he noticed a pattern in the sightings and their timings. If he could predict where and when the ghost would appear, he would keep all of his guests happy.

He found that January through March, room number 3 was haunted every other night. April through June, room number 4 was haunted every third night. July through September, room number 9 was visited by a ghost every fourth night. He then needed to plan which room would be visited in the last quarter of the year and the frequency. How did he work this out and what was his answer?

See answer 40

Uneasy Peace

The warring clans of the Campbells and the McPhersons were brought together by a marriage between the son and daughter of the opposing leading factions. The clan members, however, were still very patriotic to their own clan and were very suspicious of the opposing clan. For the first few years all activities between the clans had an equal number from each clan in the teams of workers. This covered building homes, hunting, fishing, cooking etc..

On one fateful day the fishing boat, which had a crew of 30 (15 from each clan, and headed by the Campbell leader), ran into a very bad storm and the boat began to sink. The head of the expedition agreed with the crew that half of them would have to take a risk and swim for shore in order to save the boat and the remaining crew. The head man said that he would be fair in the selection of those to leave, and that he would line everyone up in a single line formed in a circle and every ninth person would have to go. The crew agreed, and each was allotted a position numbered 1 through 30.

How did he line them up so that only the McPhersons were left?

See answer 2

The Strong Swimmer

A good swimmer jumped from his boat in the middle of the Mediterranean Sea. He swam only 100 feet from his boat and then he sank and drowned. What caused this?

Clues
1. He did not have cramp or any physical or mental health problems.
2. The waves were very light and had no bearing on the tragedy.
3. No third party was involved and his death was not because of an attack by sharks, pirates, etc.
4. He did not get tangled in any nets or weeds.
5. No other swimmer would have survived in his place.
6. The water may have been a few degrees warmer where he sank.

See answer 45

Brother Simon

Brother Simon was a monk of an order that no longer exists. He does, however, have a new job, which ensures that the old monastery collects thousands of dollars each year from tourists. After tourists are shown into his old cell the doors are locked with all of the tourists still in the cell. There is a small window, which is too small to get through, but Brother Simon manages to get out every time. How does he do it?

Clues

1. He does not have a key and the lock is not picked. The door is not opened.
2. The walls are solid with no loose stones.
3. He does not go up or down to escape the room.
4. The room warms up when he leaves the room.
5. I would not go into the room with Brother Simon.

See answer 19

The King is in his All-Together!

We have all heard the song about the king and the magic clothes that only the most intelligent people could see, but did you know that this has since been tested in the opposite direction?
A crowd of people who watched a parade saw all of the people in the parade without clothes on. They were all wearing clothes at the time. How was this accomplished?

Clues
1. No hypnosis.
2. No tricks of light or use of special glasses.
3. No use of x-rays.
4. The crowd were not related to Superman.
5. They did not undress or pass by twice.

See answer 82

Lottery Winners

This week's lottery was won by a syndicate of 10 people. Between them they won $2,775,000. They all contributed different amounts into the syndicate and their winnings were calculated against their contributions. If the amounts were all different but the cash differences between each step remained uniform, what amount did the second-highest winner get given that the sum of the lowest three amounts was equal to the sum of the top two amounts?

See answer 67

Antony & Cleopatra

One of the guards at a Roman estate found Antony and Cleopatra dead a few feet away from each other at the end of the day. He immediately called Caesar who confirmed that they were both dead. Caesar ruled out poison and there was no sign of foul play. He did see a small crack in the floor, which ran between the two bodies, and concluded that the crack caused their death. He was right, but how did they die?

Clues

1. They had not been strangled or suffocated.
2. They were both naked.
3. They were both good swimmers.
4. They did not injure themselves by diving into an empty bath or swimming pool.

See answer 36

Nylon Ball-Bearings

A factory made millions of tiny ball-bearings made from a nylon polymer. These were incredibly tough and light in weight. This made them very cheap. When a few dozen were put on a concrete floor they could support a truck without failing to work as they should. They were stored in very large wood compartments, which were 15 feet deep. Under normal circumstances the material used is quite safe and not poisonous. The death of a worker was viewed rather differently by the coroner. Why?

Clues
1. He was not killed in the manufacturing process.
2. He did not fall as a result of ball-bearings being used.
3. Nothing hit him or crushed him.
4. His death was not caused by toxic fumes from the material or as a result of fire.

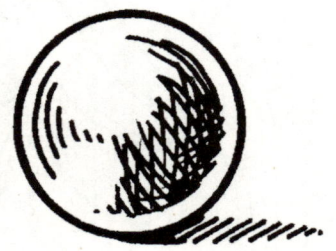

See answer 6

Levitating Balloons?

A family had inflated several different-sized balloons with air and tied the ends so that they would not deflate. These were left all over their front-room floor before they went out shopping. When they returned and looked into their front room from outside the house, they were surprised to see that all of the balloons were two inches above the floor. Why was this?

Clues

1. The room and the balloons were at the same temperature and all of the doors were firmly closed. The doors had draught excluders fitted.
2. The balloons did not contain any gases that were lighter than air.
3. The balloons were not held up by strings and no shock wave was involved.
4. Static electricity or electric charges were not the cause.
5. The cause was not air circulation.

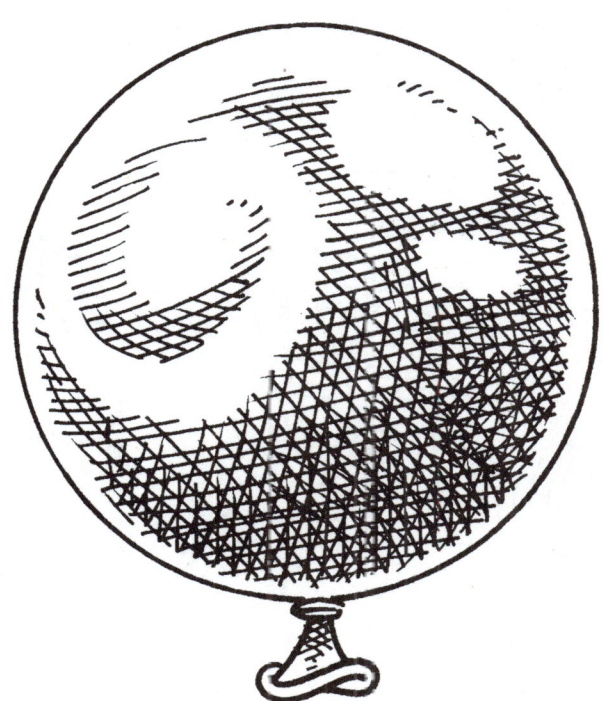

See answer 28

Trackside Jo

Trackside Jo had been taken into hospital for a serious heart condition. The nurse who looked after him noticed that he had several betting slips in his pocket when he was admitted but she thought that these should be kept from him until he was well. The extra stress, she thought, might upset his recovery. After two weeks of total rest following his operation, the nurse gave him the daily newspaper and gave him his betting slips and wallet. Looking at his first betting slip and newspaper, he noted that his first horse had won at 50-to-1 and he had $50 to win on it. When he left hospital his first call was to collect his winnings of $2500. They refused to pay him, but do you know why?

Clues

1. There was no time restriction on the betting slip.
2. The bet was valid and he had paid $50.
3. The bookmaker had not disappeared or gone bust.
4. He did not owe $2500, or more, to the bookmaker.
5. He had not made a mistake when filling out his betting slip.
6. The horse had won and was not subject to disqualification.

See answer 55

LATERAL THINKING

No Fire for Explorers

Neil and Dave were exploring a new territory. They felt a little cold and decided it was time to build a fire from some newspapers and dry bits of wood, which they had brought with them. The matches were all unused and dry, but would not light the wooden part of the match; their lighters would not work even though they seemed as though they should, and they even resorted to flintsparks and using the sun's powerful rays through a strong magnifying glass. Nothing worked. Why?

Clues
1. They were above ground and in the open.
2. There were no winds or draughts.
3. It was not wet or humid.
4. The newspaper was not wet or damp.
5. All of the equipment used to light the fire was in perfect condition.

See answer 98

King-Elect

The king had died some time ago and the queen replaced him on the throne as Head of State. They had two children who were twins. Both were delivered at birth by caesarean section, and both were born at exactly the same time.

A king had to be chosen. One of the two was very intelligent and loved by everyone, but the other was not so bright. He was not liked at all, and was not favored by the queen or people in their parliament. It was the latter who was chosen. Can you work out why?

Clues

1. There were no corrupt motives involved.
2. The constitution was used to elect the king.
3. The intelligent child did not die and was not harmed or locked away.
4. The queen agreed with the decision.
5. Foreign powers were not involved.
6. Marriage did not form part of the decision.

See answer 76

Problems with Air Pollution

A chemical plant had a major fire, which was so ferocious that it lasted 12 hours before the fire department got it under control. The police had to evacuate all of the houses within a one-mile radius because the fumes were so toxic that they would kill anyone who inhaled them within minutes. The wind initially blew the toxic gases from the west toward the east, and the wind blew constantly for 3 hours and 20 minutes. The police, however, started to clear the houses on the west of the plant because this seemed to make a great deal of sense. This evacuation procedure saved thousands of lives, but then the wind changed to blow from the east toward the west. Those who had not been evacuated either died or had serious medical problems. The wind continued to blow in this direction until the fire was completely extinguished. Only those people living to the west of the plant died. Why?

Clues

1. It did not rain.
2. Deadly toxic fumes were released all the time.
3. The toxic fumes were heavier than air and did not go over and beyond the one-mile danger circle in the east.
4. Nobody in the east had breathing apparatus and none was evacuated.
5. Closing doors and windows did not give total protection.

See answer 101

Happy New Year and Again and Again etc.

It is August and a 26-year-old woman said that she had never missed a New Year celebration in her life. She also claimed to have seen "The New Year" in 51 times. How could she be telling the truth if she was born in June?

Clues

1. She only counted January the First as a New Year and other religious or cultural New Years were not counted.
2. She did not cheat by winding her clock back.
3. Her 26 years were using a modern calendar and she lived in modern times on the planet Earth.

See answer 44

Head-On Ant Crash?

A rod of steel has a line painted on it from one end to the other. It is then twisted in the middle so that the line is half on one side and half on the opposite side. The line is painted only as wide as a quarter of an ant's width. These ants are intelligent and they are told that they must remain on the line or perish. The ants are placed at either end of the rod and told to go to the other end of the rod where they will be fed in safety. If they meet each other, they will both be killed. How do the ants resolve this problem and achieve their goals?

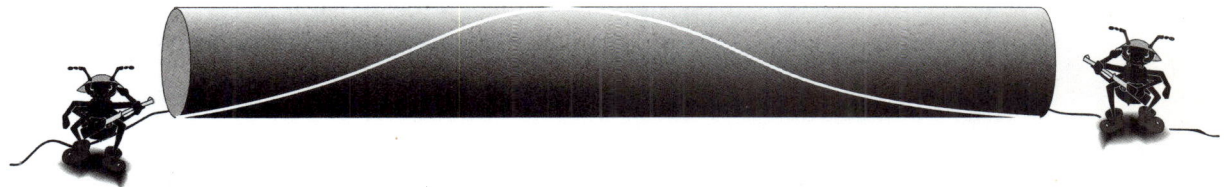

Clues

1. The rod was solid and could not be made hollow.
2. The ants could not avoid each other if they were both on the line. They could not jump over each other.
3. Both ants were fed and neither died.
4. The rod was not suspended or spun round.

See answer 8

Sinking Robots

Mission control had calculated everything down to the last detail. Experiments conducted on the planet ZOD on a previous visit showed that the mobile robots would be able to walk on ZOD's surface. The spacecraft was, however, blown off course and was forced to land on a planet similar in size to ZOD. The two robots were ejected before the crash landing and were not damaged in the descent to the surface. They then sank below the level of the surface and could not move. What caused this?

Clues

1. The soil make-up was the same on both planets and the soil density on the crust of both planets was the same.
2. They did not land on wet ground or water.
3. They did not sink because of impact speed on landing.
4. If they had ejected over ZOD they would not have sunk.

See answer 16

St. Joseph's Church

Daniel's family were very religious and always went to church on Sundays. Daniel's father had been asked to relocate because of a job promotion and they moved the family to a new city on the Saturday. The move was difficult and took all day and all of the family, except Daniel, slept in on the Sunday morning. Daniel felt tired but decided he would find his local church and thank God for the safe move straightaway, and he would lead the others to church a little later in the day. The sign outside the church said St Joseph's Catholic Church. He entered to find a service was being conducted but he did not understand a word that was being said. Why?

Clues

1. It was nothing to do with accents.
2. They had not moved to a country outside the USA.
3. Daniel was only 10 years old.
4. The language used in the church was English and not Latin.
5. He did not have a problem with his ears. He could hear everything that was said
6. The city they moved to was Washington.

See answer 88

The Rejected Recruit

Bright Sam was desperate to work in electronics for the Army. He was one of the brightest people in his class and excelled in electronics theory. When he failed to get into his chosen trade in the Army he was devastated. He knew that he was best qualified yet the Army did not want him. He later received a letter from the Army offering him a job that could save his colleagues' lives, a job that would involve him using his special gift. Can you work out what this was based on the clues given below?

Clues

1. He could not do electronics or signals because he was color-blind.
2. He was physically fit and intelligent.
3. His vision was very good, other than his problem with colors.
4. He was young and ideal for combat.

See answer 5

The Great Soccer Player Retires

A great player who had given his club and country years of good service was honored by being given a testimonial soccer match between his club and his country. It was to be his last game before retirement. The match score was 3-2 and he had scored four goals but finished on the losing team. Can you work out what happened if:

Clues

1. He scored all of his goals at one end of the stadium.
2. The winning goal was an own goal and it had not been scored by him.
3. He turned around at half-time to play in the opposite direction from the way he played in the first half.

See answer 70

The Deadwood Stagecoach

In the days of the Wild West a prospector was planning to go on the morning stagecoach to take him back east. He had struck gold and decided to celebrate in style. That evening he had drunk enough whiskey to make him drunk twice over. In the morning he found himself on the stagecoach, but it would not take him back east. Why was this?

Clues

1. He had a valid ticket and money for the trip.
2. He was on the stagecoach well before anyone else.
3. Other people wanted to go back east but nobody stopped them.
4. There was plenty of room for him on the stagecoach.
5. It was not a dangerous trip.
6. The driver for the stagecoach and the horses left on time.

See answer 34

Racetrack Confusion

On the second row of a racetrack starting grid, the driver of car number 7 was the son of the driver in car 3. They had both clocked the same third-fastest qualifying time. The driver in car 3 was not the father of the driver in car 7. How was this possible if he was also not the father-in-law or natural father?

See answer 1

Little Breeders

A man went to a pet shop and asked for a pair of budgerigars for breeding purposes. The shopkeeper sold him a pair of birds who seemed inseparable in the shopkeeper's cage. Six months later the man revisited the shop to complain that no eggs had been produced. The shopkeeper wished to keep the customer happy and gave him another budgerigar that had just laid eggs and reared the young. Six months later, the man returned again with a story of disappointing failure. Why did the hen birds fail to lay a fertile egg?

Clues

1. There was nothing wrong with any of the birds.
2. They had the right diet.
3. They were all at an age that was right for breeding.
4. It was a quiet and peaceful house.

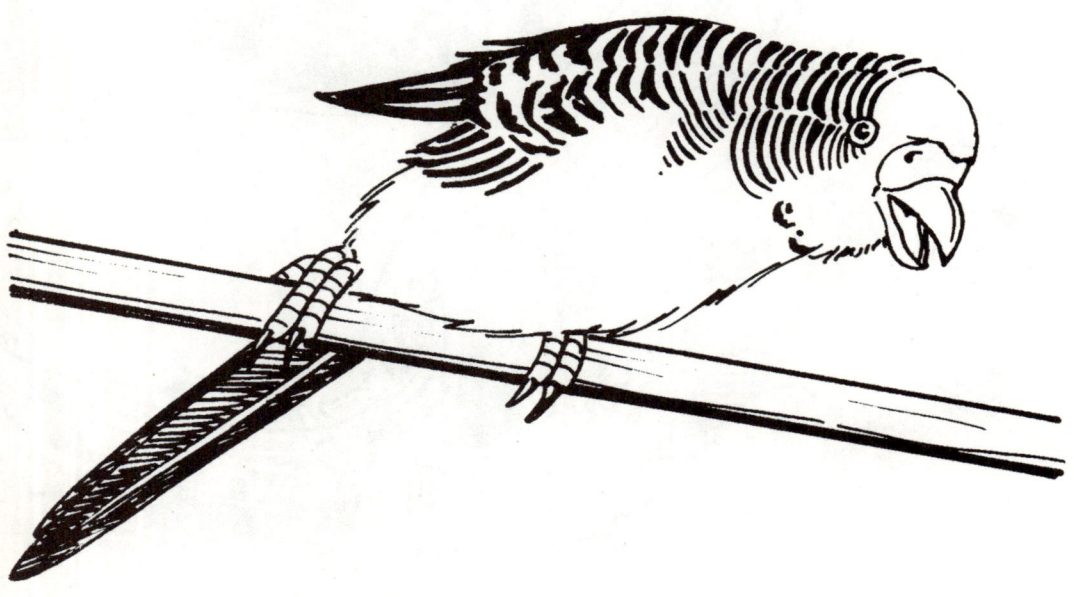

See answer 26

Who is the Bigger Liar?

In a prison a bag of sugar went missing from the kitchen. You are told in their statements that four of the five main suspects have told one lie and the other suspect has told two lies. The culprit is the person who has told two lies. Can you work this out given the following statements:

Prisoner A : I was in my cell with prisoner D and I could see prisoner B in the workshop, prisoner C in the showers, and I could also see prisoner E in the gym from either the cell door or cell window.

Prisoner B : I was in the workshop and I saw prisoner D in the gym. I also saw prisoner E in the gym and prisoner C was having a shower. I did not see prisoner A look at me through his window but he may have been in his cell.

Prisoner C : I was having a shower but I did see prisoners A and D in their cell, and also saw prisoner E in the gym. I could not see the people in the workshop.

Prisoner D : I was not with prisoner A in the cell, but I saw prisoner B in the yard watching prisoner C in the shower, and he was also watching prisoner E working out in the gym.

Prisoner E : I looked in prisoner A's cell and he was not there, but prisoner D was. Prisoner B was in the workshop and prisoner C was in the shower following a workout in the gym with me. He left me to complete my exercises.

See answer 54

Leaky Pipe

A pipe sprung a leak on its underside so that it leaked 5 gallons of water per hour until the pipe was empty 4 hours later. The leak was not detected and the pipe was refilled but a second leak, of exactly the same size, occurred immediately. The pipe was now leaking at a rate of 10 gallons of water per hour but this time it took 3 hours to empty. Can you understand why?

See answer 92

The Bus Drivers

Two bus drivers sit chatting in the staff canteen. One of the drivers leaves the canteen to meet a young boy waiting outside. A third bus driver entering the canteen asks the driver with the young boy who the boy is. "He's my son," replies the bus driver. The third bus driver sits down in the canteen and hears the other driver in there claiming that the boy is his son too. How can this be? The boy does not have any step-parents and both bus drivers are telling the truth.

No Clues : This one is quite easy.

See answer 75

The Bouquet of Flowers

A florist is making up bouquets using roses, carnations, and chrysanthemums. Twice as many of the bouquets contain carnations only as chrysanthemums only. There is one more bouquet containing roses only than carnations only. There is one more bouquet containing all three types of flowers than a mixture of roses and carnations only. There are exactly the same number of bouquets containing roses only as a mixture of carnations and chrysanthemums only. There is one more bouquet containing both roses and chrysanthemums only than containing chrysanthemums only. Two bouquets contain chrysanthemums only and 18 do not contain any chrysanthemums.

1. How many bouquets contain roses only?
2. How many bouquets contain only two of the three types of flowers?
3. How many bouquets contain carnations only?
4. How many bouquets contain all three types of flowers?
5. How many bouquets does the florist make in total?

See answer 108

Charged by a Bull

Four ramblers walked down the lane, past the stream, over the hills to the edge of a field. The field was full of cattle. Before the ramblers managed to reach the other side of the field they were charged by a bull. Why did the ramblers make a formal complaint when none of them suffered an injury?

Clues
1. They did not run to safety.
2. They were not scared.
3. The cattle took no notice of the ramblers.
4. Bulls had charged others in the past but not for a period of time.
5. The charging bull was fully fit and fully grown.

See answer 48

The Fan

A young boy going to an important soccer match decided to paint his face green, the color of his favorite team. His team won the match and he celebrated for hours with his friends after the game. When he got home he was dismayed to discover that his face was blue and not green. Why?

Clues

1. He was not painted a second time.
2. The paint was not affected by ultraviolet light.
3. The paint did not dry to blue when it was applied.
4. The paintbrush was clean and had no chemicals on it.
5. The change was not a result of temperature-sensitive or light-sensitive additives.

See answer 106

Big Bill

Big Bill was extremely tired one evening so he turned the light off and got into bed. The next morning he awoke to hear on the radio of a terrible tragedy that happened in the early hours of that morning, killing over 100 people, and it was all his fault. Why? He did not wake up and he did not sleepwalk.

Clues

1. The weather outside was bad, with poor visibility.
2. Bill was tired as he had not slept the previous night or through the day.
3. His alarm bell had been broken and it no longer rang.
4. If he had done the same things the night before, more people would probably have died.

See answer 17

Bush Fire

There was a forest fire in Australia. After the firefighters had managed to extinguish the fire, the search for bodies began. After two days of searching they found a man in complete scuba diving gear. Although he was dead, he had not been burned at all. The forest is 20 miles from any water. How did he get there?

Clues

1. The man had not walked to where he was found.
2. The man had not been murdered. It was an accidental death.
3. His wet suit was not burned or melted.
4. The man had several broken bones.

See answer 83

The Arabian Prince's Car

The Arabian prince bought a top-of-the-range car with white leather seats, state-of-the-art hi-fi, television, and every extra imaginable. It was his pride and joy to own such a car. When he got it he found that it had that 'new' smell so he stuck an air freshener on to the top of the front windscreen, and it dangled from the sucker by means of a string. After only one hour the perfume from the air freshener gave the car a beautiful smell, and the prince was very happy. He decided to drive to his father's palace in the desert to show him his delight. He left a newspaper on the dashboard and a present on the back seat for his father. A guard was posted to look after the car. His father was out but returned 2 hours later to find his son in the palace waiting for him. He rushed his father into the courtyard to find the car on fire and the guard throwing water over it. What caused the fire?

Clues

1. The fire started inside the passenger section of the car.
2. No electrical or fuel problems existed.
3. The present did not contain any flammable materials.
4. Firearms and matches were not involved.
5. Spontaneous combustion was not the cause.
6. It had nothing to do with chemicals in the air freshener.
7. The guard had nothing to do with the cause of the fire.

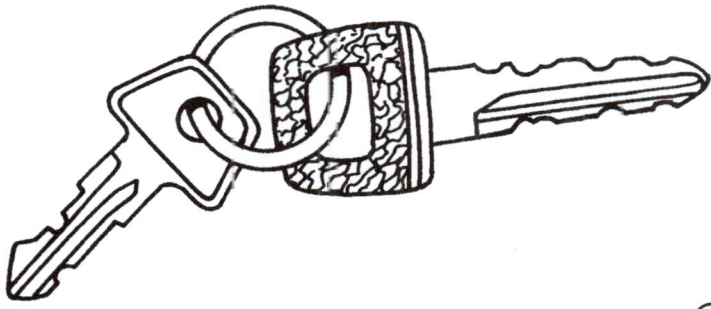

See answer 64

Moving Suitcases

A family on vacation in Florida returned to their rented apartment one day only to see their empty suitcases placed at the side of the road almost 2 miles from the apartment. They stopped their car and inspected the cases, which had their names on the name labels. Why had their suitcases been placed at the side of the road?

Clues

1. They had paid their rent and still had one week's rent paid in advance.
2. They had been away for the day.
3. They had not been burgled.
4. The landlords did not have the suitcases removed.
5. They had left the suitcases in the apartment before leaving for the day.

See answer 37

Amateur Safe-Crackers

Two cowboys, Lightfingers Harry and Desperate Dave, decided that they would blow open the safe in the town bank, which contained many thousands of dollars. They had never blown a safe before but they knew where they could get as much gunpowder as they might need. Over a drink in the saloon they asked a drunk gold prospector how much gunpowder they would need. He told them about 2 pounds, but Desperate Dave insisted that they used twice the amount to make sure. They entered the bank, poured the gunpowder, and lit the fuse. The safe did not open and not a sound was heard. Why?

Clues

1. All of the gunpowder was used and it ignited. The powder was dry and they used all 4 pounds.
2. They did not try to soundproof the room and it was not soundproofed already. People were nearby.
3. The powder was placed on and around the safe, close enough to get the job done

See answer 41

The Immovable Screw

A man decided to repair his wife's vacuum cleaner (much to her despair, since he had shown no aptitude with electrical or mechanical problems in the past). The first job was to remove the screws using his screwdriver. He ensured that the right size and type of point on the screwdriver matched the screw head perfectly. He then engaged the screwdriver to the screw head, applied the necessary force, and turned the handle anti-clockwise. The screw would not come out and it would not loosen. Why?

Clues

1. The pressure applied by the husband was adequate to remove the screw.
2. Turning the screw anti-clockwise was the correct way to loosen and remove the screw.
3. Good contact between the screw and screwdriver was maintained. The screwdriver did not slip off the screw head.
4. The thread in the hole did not get stripped and the screw was not damaged or deformed.
5. His wife was able to undo the screws without any problems using the same screwdriver and without lubricants.

See answer 27

The Tea Party

A mother calls her daughter to come and play in the house. The little girl comes running through the front door and decides to have a tea party with her dolls and teddy bears. After half an hour she is bored with this game, and decides to go back outside to play with her ball in the front garden. To get to the front garden she has to go through two front doors. Why?

Clues
1. The house does not have a porch door.
2. One front door is facing the back wall of the house.

See answer 56

Two Brothers

In 1914 there were two brothers of an aristocratic family in England. When war broke out the first brother volunteered for the army without delay. After basic training he was sent to the front line. He was an officer and led his unit with complete distinction for over 12 months. Upon his return for a rest he went to his family home to find his brother just having a good time. For generations his family had served their country with honor, but his brother was bringing shame on the family name. The officer returned to the front and suffered an injury; while in the hospital he sent a letter to his brother, which caused his brother to enlist as a foot-soldier and win medals of distinction and bravery. The letter sent did not contain a letter or any words from his brother. Yet he knew by what was in there what it meant. What was in the letter?

Clues

1. The handwriting on the envelope was not his brother's.
2. It had a postmark that could not be read.
3. His brother did not speak to him to cause him to change his mind.
4. The envelope contained something that weighed no more than the envelope itself.
5. There was no message on the envelope.

See answer 95

The Bath of Liquid

A man fell into a full bath of liquid at work. When he got out he was dry, but he was taken straight to a hospital. Can you explain why he was dry and why he was taken to hospital?

Clues

1. The liquid in the bath was at room temperature.
2. There were warning signs to keep clear.
3. It was an accident that caused him to fall into the bath.
4. He had fallen gently and had not suffered a concussion or any severe blows.
5. The liquid in the bath was 4 feet deep, and little was lost when he fell in.
6. He was not wearing any protective clothing.
7. He had not ingested any of the liquid.
8. He was required to burn his clothes.

See answer 77

Car Park Overcrowding

A company had a car park where all of the 10 spaces were allocated to its managers. They expanded the business and a new manager joined them. Part of his contract was to have a car-park space, just like the other managers. How was this achieved if nobody was asked to double-park?

Clues

1. The cars could not obstruct either of the access roads.
2. All of the spaces between the cars had to remain the same.
3. The extra car could not be parked in a location away from the front office wall, and all of the other managers kept their slot.
4. All of the cars needed to be parked at the same time.

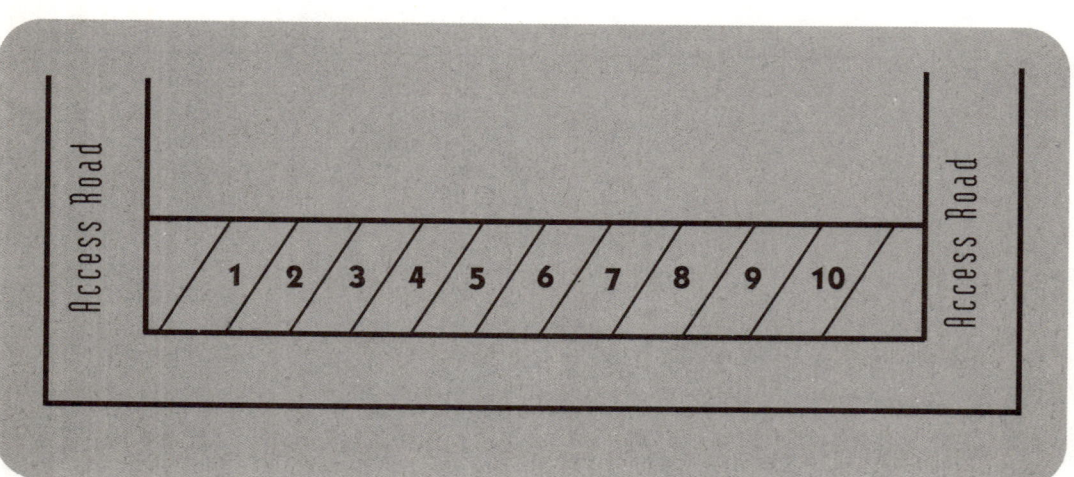

See answer 109

The Courier's Wait

The courier phoned his customer to say that the crate that he had brought with him weighed one ton, and that they would need lifting equipment to unload it. He was less than a mile from the delivery point but it would be 6 hours before he could get there. He had covered the 20 miles from the collection point in just over one hour. Why would it take so much longer to reach the delivery point given the following clues?

Clues

1. He was not taking a detour, and there was no traffic between his current position and the delivery point.
2. He was not being held up because of other meetings or people.
3. The delay was not caused by unloading or loading any other products.
4. If it was $5^3/_4$ hours later, he could make the same journey in 15 minutes.
5. The roads in the area were free from traffic congestion and road works.
6. The reason was not due to anything anyone did.

See answer 23

Leap to Safety

A man sleeping on the top floor of a three-storey house awakes to find smoke coming under his bedroom door. He gathers as many of his treasured possessions as he can possibly hold and leaps out of the bedroom window. Even though his arms are full, he doesn't drop or break anything and he does not injure himself. Why?

Clues

1. Some of the items were fragile and would have broken if they had hit the ground.
2. He did not jump on to a ledge on the house.
3. No ladders, ropes, or safety nets were employed.
4. He did not jump into water or soft snow.

See answer 50

The Class

James trudges off to school each morning with his books but he rarely does homework, and he doesn't achieve high marks in tests either. There are 36 children in his class and 35 of them are good students. Why does James never get into trouble?

Clues

1. James is always polite
2. James has been sent to the head's office on a number of occasions.
3. James is not related to anyone at the school and he is not a special student.

See answer 20

A Fruity Problem

A woman has a small collection of artificial fruits on the windowsill. The apple is rosy red on one side and bright green on the other side, and there is a little white stalk sticking out from the top. The peach is a lovely soft warm shade of pinky-orange, with a larger white stalk. There is also a pear and a deep burgundy-colored plum. The woman leaves them on the windowsill and goes out of the room. When she returns half an hour later she cannot see the fruits at all. Why? Nobody else has been in the room. Nobody has moved them. There is nothing blocking her view; the room is clear, and there is no mist.

Clues

1. They had not been stolen.
2. They had not been eaten.
3. A telltale clue had been left.
4. The room had an unusual smell about it when she returned.
5. Animals and insects had nothing to do with the disappearance.

See answer 85

Disappearing Treat

At a candy store a young boy was allowed to choose what he wanted. He came out of the shop happily clutching a full bag. He made a hole in the top of the bag and began eating. He only ate a small amount of the contents but within half an hour his bag was virtually empty. He did not drop the bag or its contents. He did not give any away, throw any away, or transfer the contents into anything else. Where did the contents of the bag go?

Clues

1. Only about 5% of the content of the bag had been consumed.
2. The hole in the bag did not let any of the contents out.
3. The contents were not eaten by insects or anything else.

See answer 39

The Messy Eater

Much to his colleagues' annoyance, Arthur brought fruit to the office each day for his lunch. He would peel his banana and leave the skin lying around, drop apple cores all over the floor, spit the pips from his grapes over other peoples' desks, and he was forever squirting people in the eye with his orange. Arthur still brings fruit to work but no longer gets complaints from his colleagues. He has not changed his habits, he has not done or said anything to his colleagues, and his colleagues have not changed. Why does he no longer get complaints?

Clues

1. He did not work with animals and the office was normally a clean environment.
2. He no longer used his fingers to hold the fruit.

See answer 63

The Fabric Shop

In a curtain shop there are flowered fabrics hanging up in the section marked 'Floral Designs'. All the curtains in various colors but with no pattern on them are in the section marked 'Plain Fabrics'. Why are a pair of curtains with continuous vertical lines down them not in the section marked 'Striped Fabrics'?

Clues

1. There was a section marked 'Striped Fabrics'.
2. They were vertical stripes.
3. They had not been misplaced in another section.
4. The customers knew where to find the curtains they needed.

See answer 35

The Disappearing Man

One cold winter morning Jayne was walking down a narrow country lane. On either side of the lane there were four houses. Jayne noticed that each house had a different-colored front door and different-colored cars parked in the driveways. Outside one of the houses she noticed a man standing in the garden. He was very well dressed with a hat and scarf on to keep him warm. She waved at the gentleman and shouted, "Hello!" and he smiled at her. Later that day when she came back along the lane she noticed the man again. She waved to him and said, "It certainly is getting warmer, it doesn't feel as cold as it was this morning." The gentleman smiled at her and she went on her way, counting the cars that passed her as she went. The next day when Jayne went down the lane she noticed the gentleman had gone. Where?

Clues

1. He had not gone inside the house or any other house.
2. He had not walked down the lane in any direction.
3. He had not driven anywhere by car.

See answer 7

Washing Dishes

A married couple in New York had six children and each night of the week one child would wash the dishes. This task was performed by a different child every night. On Sundays all of the children would draw lots to see who would have the sad privilege. One of the children figured that it was best to be left the last lot and not pick at all. She calculated that the first pick would have a 1 : 5 choice, the next a 1 : 4 choice, the next 1 : 3, etc until she was left with the last lot. The child added all of the previous factors together and decided that it would be unlikely that it would be the worst lot left. Was this trick likely to work?

See answer 29

1930s

On one early transatlantic flight in the 1930s a plane carrying 20 passengers had very low fuel reserves when approaching New York from England. It was a very windy day when the plane arrived, but it could not land where it was supposed to because of the wind. It was, however, able to land only a few miles away where the wind had a slightly higher speed. Why was this possible?

Clues

1. The wind direction for landing at the second landing point was less favorable. It was more of a crosswind than the wind at the first landing point.
2. The first arrival area had no other vehicles on it and no other air traffic was involved.
3. Air traffic control did not advise of anything being wrong with the plane, and indeed nothing was wrong with the plane.
4. The plane was not diverted because of the low fuel situation.
5. The pilot could see why he should divert the plane.

See answer 57

Dangerous Neighbors?

The Price family were regarded by their neighbors in Quietsville as complete undesirables. At least one of the family would always be terrorizing some neighbor. The neighbors were too frightened to speak to the police because of their fear of reprisals based on a long history of previous events. One day the situation escalated into a much more serious problem when one of the Price family set fire to a neighbor's home. The police questioned all of the neighbors, but even though some knew who did the deed they would not say. One neighbor handed a note to a policeman, and he went straight to the right member of the family. If the family names were Mr Tom Price (father), Mrs Julie Price (mother), and the children were James, David, Mark, and Chuck, which family member was arrested?

See answer 96

The Last Train

Mr Punctual was not, as his name suggested, always punctual. One day he had to work late in the office and needed to rush to the train station to catch the last train home. He ran on to the station to the normal platform only to see a train leaving the station. Not having looked at his watch, he did not know if it was the 9.55pm train. A quick glance at his watch confirmed that it could not have been his train. How did he know this?

Clues

1. His watch was showing the correct time.
2. He did not ask anyone any questions.
3. He had not read anything about delays.
4. His train was on time and had not been re-scheduled.

See answer 74

The Unlucky Locksmith

A locksmith was called to an exclusive bank and asked to change the lock on a room that was used to store valuable documents. The door was to be activated only by the breaking of two low-power laser beams in front of the door. This would release a steel plate that covered the lock, and the owner could then use the new special key to open the lock. The system was to be automatic and re-set itself after use. Just before he had completed his clearing up, the manager of the bank wanted to check it out and after helping the locksmith to clear his tools from the storeroom, he was locked into the storeroom. The locksmith could not get him out. Why?

Clues

1. The door had closed by accident or by design.
2. The police and fire department had to release the manager.
3. The locksmith had to change the lock again.
4. The locksmith still had the key but he could not make it work, even though he had tested it before clearing up.
5. The laser beams were only 3 feet apart.

See answer 105

The Glass Head

In recognition of the President's services to his country and for his contribution to world peace, a huge, two-ton polished glass head of his likeness was commissioned, the base of which was to be flat to ensure that it did not move on its plinth. The top of the plinth matched the neck of the glass head perfectly. An overhead crane with specially padded ropes was used to lift the head on to the neck, but then a problem occurred. The two parts had to be positioned exactly, and the workers could not drag the ropes, since this would chip the head or base. How did they do it?

Clues

1. They could not use wooden wedges or anything that might scratch the glass.
2. They could not use compressed air since the compressor did not have the power.
3. The ropes had to pass under the neck in 4 places.
4. The ropes were made of nylon, which covered a stainless steel core. They were 2 inches in diameter.
5. They could not use suckers or rubber props.

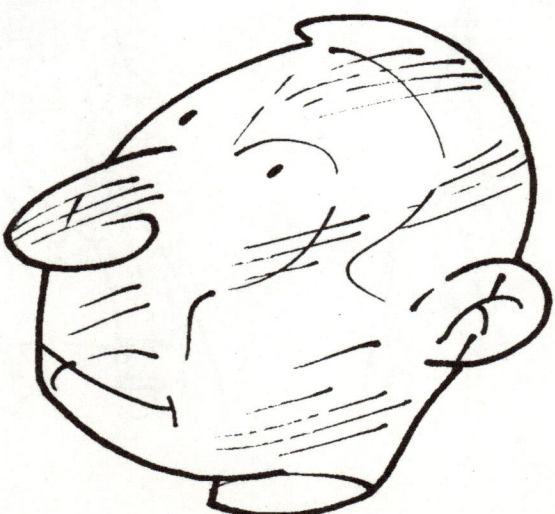

See answer 115

Survival of the Weakest?

Three men were passionately in love with a lady. The woman loved them all equally, but the passion boiled over and the men agreed that they should have a duel using pistols. To the victor, the hand of the lady; to the vanquished and defeated, death, injury, or disappointment.

After agreeing to duel, the odds were stacked against one and in favor of the other two. As Count Nevermiss was an expert and a perfect shot, he had won every duel even against better opposition than he was to face that fateful day. Lord Bullseye was a good shot and a military man. He could be relied on to hit his target two out of every three shots, while Captain Missalot could only be relied upon to hit his target once every three shots. They were, however, men of honor and decided that the rules of the duel gave the poorer shots a chance. They decided that they would stand and face each other from three points of a triangle. There was no limit to ammunition, but they would shoot in turn at either of the opponents with the worst shot going first and the best shot shooting last.

You are put in Captain Missalot's position. How do you maximize your chances of survival with honor? It is you who will shoot first. Who are you going to go for? Survival depends on good lateral and deductive reasoning.

See answer 42

A Problem for the Ferryman

A man leaves his 5 children with the ferryman and is told that they must all be taken to the other side of the river in a minimum number of crossings, such that each of the children has an identical number of one-way trips. The children are all of different ages and the ferryman can only take himself plus a maximum of 2 children at any time. No pair of children of neighboring ages can be left in the absence of the ferryman. Only the ferryman can row the boat. How many trips are needed and what is the sequence?

See answer 18

Household Enquiry

A man enters his house. He asks his daughter, Sally, a question (to which he does not know the answer). The question is such that whatever the answer, right, wrong, true or false, he will know the answer to his question. What was the question?

Clues
1. His daughter did not have prior knowledge of the question.
2. She could have answered with any word or words.
3. She was not in the room when the question was asked.

See answer 84

The Puzzle King of Egypt

Long ago in the days of the Pharaohs the Puzzle King was a very favored man – so much so that one of the Pharaohs allowed him to design the entrance to his tomb. The Pharaoh said that his tomb must not be plundered after his death so the design had to deter his people from trying to enter. He would also have 200 of his strongest soldiers entombed with him in case he revived and needed to be released. The design for entrance is shown below. The magic cube would seal the entrance. How did the cube go together before it was moved into position in the pyramid so that the Pharaoh could get out?

Clues

1. The cube was solid and made from stone. It was made in two halves as shown.
2. Dovetail joints were on the faces that you cannot see and are in central positions. The cube looks the same from each side view. Each side has the same dovetail joint showing.
3. 200 men could move half of the cube but they would not be able to move the entire cube. It took 400 men to move the cube into place.
4. No outside help was needed.
5. No hinges or tricks were employed.

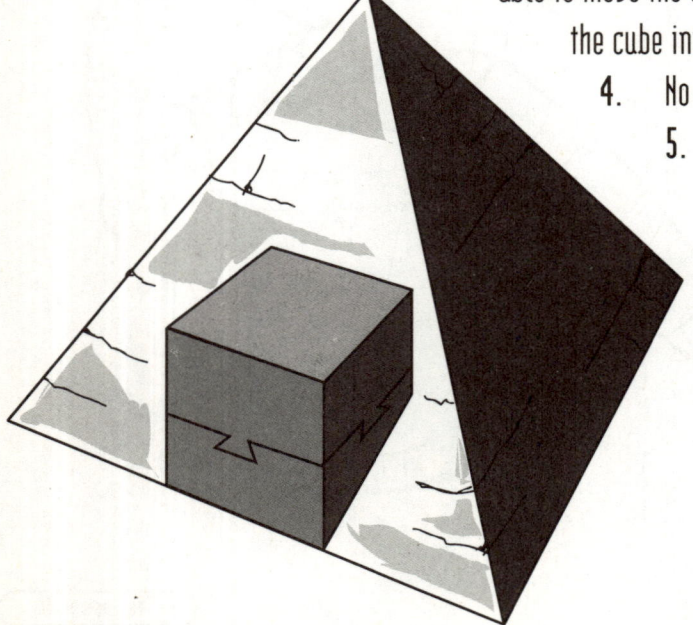

See answer 66

Target Practice

The twins Larry and Pete got up one morning and painted some large targets on the door of the barn. After the paint had dried, they found that their baseball damaged the door if they pitched a fastball. The rubber ball and tennis balls were either lost or of no use because they did not leave a mark to show where they hit the targets. The twins, who were very competitive, did have a solution, one that also pleased their parents. They threw balls at the door for hours and could accurately score every shot without leaving a mess to be cleared away later and without damaging the paintwork. How was this possible?

Clues

1. The balls had no dye and no mud.
2. The balls did not bounce.
3. The twins were told to clear the yard before they could play ball. This instruction was in their best interest.
4. The children kept clean.

See answer 32

Sally's Wash

Sally goes to the bathroom to have a wash. She wants to run a full basin of water so that she can get a nice lather on the soap, but unfortunately the plug for the basin has been lost. She cannot find another plug anywhere and cannot find anything else to fill the plughole. She knows, however, that while the water from the one faucet will not stay in the basin, the water from the other faucet will not run away. Why is this?

Clues

1. She does not jam the soap in the plughole.
2. The plughole can let out water more quickly than both faucets on full.
3. A few days before and a few days later she could not have used this idea.
4. She had to run the other faucet to clean the basin.

See answer 3

Hold-Up Clues

A man walks into a bar and asks for a glass of water. The barman goes into the back and then returns to the bar wearing a mask and holding a gun. The customer thanks him and walks out of the bar without ever having any water. Why was he satisfied?

Clues

1. The barman did not know the customer.
2. The customer was not a criminal.
3. The barman did not give or take anything from the customer, although the customer lost something.

See answer 25

The Aircraft

Why did the men fill the transatlantic passenger jet's fusilage with water?

Clues

1. It was safe to do so.
2. The jet was not on fire or a fire risk.
3. Passengers were at risk prior to this being done.
4. It was not an emergency procedure after landing on water.
5. It was not a safety drill.

See answer 51

The Inherited House

Jamie did not know his uncle had left him Sea View House when he passed away. He knew that it was a mansion built about 200 yards back from the cliffs overlooking the sea. He had been there when he was a child, some 30 years ago. Jamie was not close to his uncle, but he was the last surviving relative. It had taken legal investigators some years to find Jamie, as he worked overseas. When he saw the mansion again, he was very disappointed. Why?

Clues

1. It had been well maintained and was in good order.
2. No building had been placed between the house and the sea.
3. The gardens were still in good order.
4. The nearby town had prospered.
5. It was not sentimental disappointment.
6. His uncle had lived there until he died.

See answer 93

A Bargain

Why did the multi-millionaire decide to buy land that was over 200 yards from the seashore?

Clues
1. It was under the sea.
2. It did not contain any mineral rights and it had nothing to do with mining.
3. There was no oil for hundreds of miles.
4. It was not a port or going to be a port or harbor.
5. It had nothing to do with swimming rights.
6. It was a bargain.

See answer 71

The Fire Drill

At a school in Florida the fire bell sounded for a fire drill. The children and teachers were orderly and knew what to do. The children did not know that it was a practice session. The fire department, however, were needed because a major state of panic ensued. What occurred?

Clues

1. The teachers and children could not exit the building.
2. The Fire Department knew of the fire drill but they were not required to be on site for the drill. They were, however, summoned.
3. Many lives could have been saved by not leaving the school building.
4. Fire was not involved.
5. Doors and windows were closed throughout the school.

See answer 107

Don't Jump to Conclusions

A man was born before his father and he married his three sisters. He did nothing against the laws of God or man. How was this so?

Clues

1. He remained celibate all his life.
2. He only had one father but worshipped another.
3. He did not belong to a religious order that permitted close family or multiple marriages.
4. His father was 30 years older than he.

See answer 49

The Musical End

The entire family gathered around Grandpa's bed in the hospital at visiting time as usual. He had been in a coma for a few days but he was not expected to die in the near future. The piped music in the hospital stopped suddenly and Grandpa died almost immediately. Why?

Clues
1. He was hooked up to monitors and drip feeds.
2. He was hooked up to life-support equipment.
3. The equipment did not fail.
4. The power supply to the equipment did not fail.
5. His death was preventable.

See answer 13

A Body Bag in the Suitcase

Cheryl had just met a new boyfriend, Floyd. They met in Las Vegas and got married after a whirlwind romance. When they loaded up the car she looked into a suitcase that she had not packed, which had been left in the trunk of the car by her new husband. It contained a body bag with a boy's body in it. The suitcase had holes in it so that air could get into it and the body bag was partially open. She did not leave Floyd or report the incident to the police. Why?

Clues

1. He told her that she had found his best friend.
2. The body bag was used for protection.
3. The boy was 7 years old.
4. It was not his son.
5. The body was fully dressed.
6. Foul play was not suspected even though an arm had been broken.

See answer 89

Cardinal Lock'emup

The Cardinal was given the king's own writing desk for catching and locking up a musketeer who, it was alleged, seduced the queen. The desk was magnificent, with thousands of inlays and studded with jewels. It had 4 crystal inkwells and a drawer for 20 quills. The Cardinal, who was the Minister for Justice, knew that the musketeer was not guilty, but it suited his plans to have him executed. On the day before the scheduled execution, 3 musketeers had an audience to plead with the cardinal for leniency. The cardinal would not listen so the musketeers made him listen at the end of a sword and made him write out a release paper, which is shown below.

> To The Captain of Guards
>
> I authorize the immediate release of Musketeer Antonio.
> He is innocent of the charges made against him
>
> Signed : Cardinal Lockemup

Clues

1. The musketeers saw the letter being written.
2. The format and seals for the letter were in order.
3. The cardinal had not anticipated such a move and had not given special instructions to the Captain of Guards.
4. The king and queen did not know what was going on.
5. The musketeers did not have an arrest warrant out for them.
6. Antonio was the right musketeer and they went to the correct jail.
7. The cardinal did not raise the alarm.

The letter was sealed using the cardinal's seal, rolled up and sealed again. The cardinal was then asked to ensure that he would not be disturbed for 2 hours. He was then bound, gagged, and locked in his room. The 3 musketeers then went to collect the other musketeer and were all arrested. Why?

See answer 61

The Burglar

A burglar climbed into a house but made an unusually large amount of noise for him. He ran through the house and identified the owner's most precious treasures and ran out of the house with them. On exiting the house he found that the police were already waiting for him. The homeowners did not press charges and the police took the case no further. The neighbors who had been awakened by the commotion, however, insisted that the man be arrested. What was going on?

Clues

1. The house was alarmed.
2. The noise made by the burglar woke everyone in the house.
3. He had to get out of the house quickly.
4. He was planning to burgle the house.
5. The judge was lenient.

See answer 33

The Policewoman

The policewoman just watched as a man tried to pick a lock to enter a house. He failed to get in so he broke a window and gained access.

The policewoman was not on duty and she failed to report the crime. Why?

Clues
1. She knew the person's house.
2. She did not follow the incident up when she next went to work.
3. She liked the people living in the house.
4. She knew that the people living there were in no danger.

See answer 10

The Removal Men

The removal men had been asked to pack and move the contents of a very expensive house to another even more exclusive area. The house contents included fine silver and gold cutlery, rare pieces of art and very expensive collections of stamps. One of the removal men found the temptation too much and stole a page from the stamp collection. It was the homeowner who was jailed. How could this be?

Clues

1. It was not an insurance scam.
2. The removal man did not know the homeowner.
3. The removal man lost his job and was arrested.
4. The value of each of the stamps was over $10,000 each.

See answer 24

LATERAL THINKING

The Savage Attack

A man charged through a crowd of people and ripped off a pretty lady's blouse, punched her on the chest, and carried her away with him. The crowd were in shock and nobody tried to stop the man. Why not?

Clues
1. He had never seen the lady before.
2. The police pursued him.
3. He was not armed and was not a physically strong person.
4. The police did not arrest him.

See answer 53

Cheap Shopper!

A man on low income wanted more for his family than he could provide. He devised a scheme that he thought might help him achieve this. He was useful with a computer and understood how the supermarket system worked. After going to the supermarket he implemented his scheme. He had a full trolley of goods and was prepared to pay the price on the register for all of the goods, yet he was arrested. Why?

Clues

1. The register asked for $120.25, which he offered to pay.
2. All of the goods bought were in tins, jars, or packets. He did not buy any fruit or vegetables.
3. He had planned this very well and had not been noticed as doing anything wrong by security cameras in the store.
4. He declared everything at the register and kept nothing in the trolley or on his person.

See answer 94

Father vs Son

Joe's son was very fit and worked out every day but he was not the brainiest of individuals. Joe had seen his youth come and go and he was now in his late 40s and not in good health. He felt that he could still beat his son even if he gave his son a small start. Joe's son, who would never throw a chance to beat his father, took up the challenge, but still lost. How?

Clues

1. Joe was never any good as an athlete.
2. Joe never cheated and did not have any help.
3. It did not involve any motors or sails.
4. Joe's son did not let his father win deliberately.
5. The son had a 10-second start.

See answer 72

The Awkward Piano

Alf was a bit of a practical joker and his workmates would always be under attack from him. One day they had to move a piano and some other items up the stairs in a department store. Although the piano was heavy, they decided that they could still put a few things on top of it before they carried it up the stairs. Alf was going backward and went up the stairs at the leading edge of the piano. Joe was at the bottom end and soon ran into a problem. Alf asked if he could hold the piano in place while he got help. Joe said, "Yes, but be quick." Alf rushed off and returned in under a minute pushing something into Joe's top pocket. "There," said Alf, "that should do it!" Joe was not amused. What had Alf done that he thought might have helped Joe so much? (Not!).

Clues

1. He used a literal translation of a need for help.
2. It did not help Joe at all and the piano was stuck.
3. Nobody else helped.

See answer 104

The Fire

The couple had just finished building their home and because the night would be very cold, they wanted to build a fire to keep warm. The wind outside was gusting at 40 mph and they were soon very cozy and fell asleep. A few hours later they were both dead. What had gone wrong?

Clues
1. The home had not burned down.
2. The house had not blown down.
3. They had not suffocated.
4. They had not been burned to death.

See answer 43

Is the Doctor Wrong?

A farm worker fell from his tractor and suffered bruising and what he thought might be a broken ankle. He was taken to the local hospital where the student doctor started to investigate his problems. Almost at once he shouted, "Cardiac arrest!" and revival equipment was rushed into the out-patients area. The diagnosis was correct and the farm worker went home in the next 5 hours. How could this be?

Clues

1. The farm worker was alive when he went home and he was discharged by qualified staff.
2. The student doctor did everything correctly.
3. The consultant physician thanked the doctor for his prompt action.
4. Neither the broken ankle, nor the bruising, caused the cardiac arrest.

See answer 113

The Master Forger

The best forger of all time was indeed a most brilliant artist and a man respected and sought after in the criminal world. He was so good that every major intelligence force kept a watchful eye on him and anyone he came in contact with. They even bugged his home and workplace with microphones and cameras. This came in useful when he was asked to copy the new $50 note. The police were tipped off and decided to search his premises before he even got started. Why?

Clues

1. It was not to see if he had any paper or ink.
2. It was not to see if he had any photographic equipment.
3. The search was successful.
4. The forger made perfect copies of the $50 note at a later date and was immediately arrested and jailed.

See answer 58

Golfers

Two golfers had a challenge match. One scored 72 and the other scored 74. The player with the highest score won. How could this be given the following clues?

Clues

1. They played off the same handicap.
2. They had both scored correctly.
3. Neither player had incurred penalty shots and they followed the rules precisely.
4. The player with the lower score was not disqualified.
5. It was not a tournament where only the player scoring 74 was entered.

See answer 87

LATERAL THINKING

The Cup of Coffee

A blind man went into a restaurant and ordered a cup of coffee. When it arrived he complained that the coffee was not hot enough and requested a fresh cup. When it arrived he complained that it was in the same cup. How did he know?

Clues

1. The cup did not have a crack or anything that distinguished it from the other cups that were used in the restaurant.
2. He could not tell by the temperature of the cup.
3. He had not left a sticky mark or cream on the outside of the cup.

See answer 62

Mad Driver?

Why did the driver accelerate quickly to ram the car in front of him on the three-lane freeway?

Clues
1. He had not been drinking or taking drugs.
2. He did not know the driver in the car in front of him.
3. His foot had not had a muscle spasm; his action was deliberate.
4. He did not wish to harm anyone.
5. It was not a result of an act of nature such as an earthquake.
6. It was not to leap over a broken bridge or hole in the road.

See answer 31

Amazement

The child watched in total amazement as a man blew up a bank, killing three people. The child had a clear view of the whole event and was the only person to witness what went on. The police did not need to question him. Why?

Clues

1. The child was 12 years old.
2. The child told his parents what he had seen and they did not report it.
3. The family were not afraid of repercussions.
4. The man was not known to the child but he could describe the killer and all of the events clearly.
5. The child was not one to lie.
6. The killer did not own up to the killing.

See answer 4

Triangles

What is the largest number of non-overlapping triangles that can be produced by drawing 7 straight lines?

This diagram only gives 5 but you can get many more from 7 lines.

See answer 22

The Jealous Husbands

(This puzzle was devised in 1612 by Claude-Gaspar Bachet)

Three jealous husbands with their wives have to cross a river in a rowboat. The boat can only carry 2 people at a time, and only 3 of the 6 people can row. How can the 6 of them cross the river so that none of the women will be left in the company of any other man unless when her husband is present?

See answer 59

The Meeting

The man from Nepal came by plane to visit the man from China who wore a chain around his neck. What was the weather like when the man from Iran joined them?

See answer 99

Confusion & Lies

There was once a family that was well known for being awkward. The males in the family always told the truth but the women in the family never made two consecutive true or untrue statements.

When met by a visitor, the father and mother had one child with them. The visitor asked the child, "Are you a boy?" but the visitor could not understand the reply. One of the parents said that the child responded, "I am a boy". The other parent then said, "The child lied, she is a girl". Was the child a boy or a girl and what did the child say?

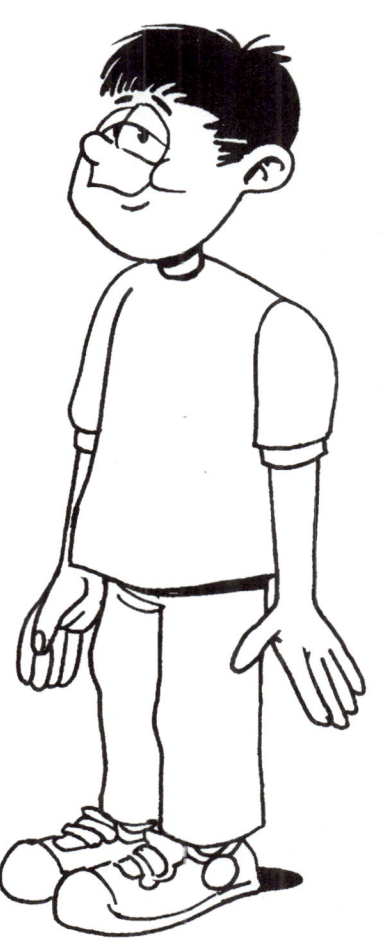

See answer 78

Lateral Thinking Gem From Times Gone By

Can you make 101010 into 950 by adding just one straight line.

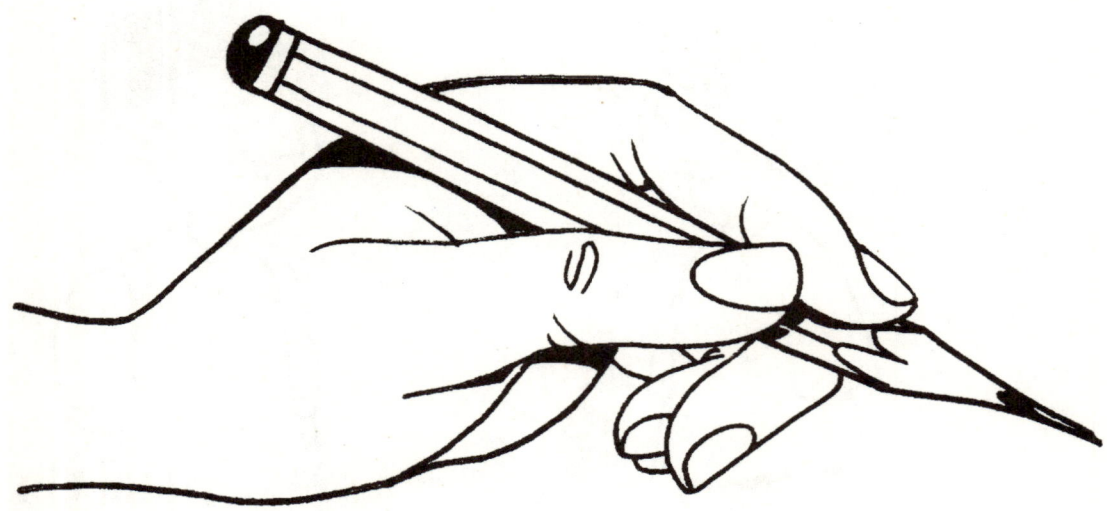

See answer 111

The Casino

Five people sat on the edge of a large casino and played from 10pm to 3am. They were professionals and did not stop for a break and nobody joined or left them. They played together without the assistance of anyone from the casino. They kept their own scores and, at the end, all of them went home with more than they had to start with. How could this be?

Clues

1. They were not playing against machines such as slot machines or blackjack machines.
2. They were not playing bingo or against the house.
3. Each of them went home not losing and always gaining. whenever they played together at the casino.

See answer 47

Corporal in the Army

A man sat down in a restaurant and started to read the menu out loud, but to himself. "Steak and fries, $7; steak, egg, and fries, $8.50; salad, $4 ..." etc. The waiter went up to the man and said, "You must be a corporal in the Army". He was correct but how did he make this connection?

Clues

1. They had not met before and the man was alone.
2. They were not near an army base.
3. The man's voice was not disturbing anyone.
4. He did not speak like a drill-sergeant.

See answer 112

The Abandoned

Charlie was abandoned at an early age and life had been a struggle, not just for him, but also for his adoptive parents. He killed his adoptive parents' offspring, yet they still worked hard to ensure he survived and had a home. As soon as Charlie was old enough he left his parents, never to return.

Neither the police nor the social services had anything to do with Charlie, even though he also killed his own offspring. Why?

Clues

1. It had nothing to do with being underage when he killed.
2. His family had a reputation for punctuality.
3. His adoptive parents did not press charges even though the murders were brutal.
4. He never joined the military or had a social service number.
5. He was born in the spring.

See answer 11

The Cheetah and the Hyena

The cheetah tells lies on Mondays, Tuesdays and Wednesdays, and tells the truth on each of the other days of the week. The hyena lies on Thursdays, Fridays and Saturdays, but tells the truth on each of the other days.

One day the lion heard them talking. The cheetah said, "Yesterday I lied all day," to which the hyena responded with exactly the same words. What day was it?

See answer 86

Lost For Days

What day is it when the day after tomorrow is yesterday and today will be as far from Sunday as today was from Sunday, when the day before yesterday was tomorrow?

See answer 65

Alien Conference

It was the year 2156AD and 1000 aliens attended the intergalactic meeting on Mars.

606 had 3 eyes.

700 had 2 noses.

497 had 4 legs.

20 had none of the above 3 traits.

4 times as many people had only 3 eyes as an oddity as had only 4 legs as an oddity.

220 aliens had a combination of all 3 oddities.

How many aliens had only 2 noses as an oddity if only 30 aliens had 3 eyes and 4 legs as oddities?

See answer 80

The Millionaire's Inheritance

A millionaire leaves $14,148,167 to his 7 sons and the rest to charity. In his will he makes a proviso that everything must be given to charity if the sons cannot divide the money equally between them. Is there a way in which they can inherit?

See answer 9

Another Mansion Murder

The Lord of the Manor has been murdered. The visitors to the manor were Abbie, Bobby and Colin. The murderer was the visitor who arrived at the manor later than at least one of the other two visitors. One of the visitors was a detective who arrived at the manor earlier than at least one of the other two visitors. The detective arrived at midnight. Neither Abbie nor Bobby arrived at the manor after midnight. The earlier arriver of Bobby and Colin was not the detective. The later arriver of Abbie and Colin was not the murderer. Who then was it who committed the murder?

See answer 21

In the Dirt

Two children were playing in the loft of a barn before it gave way and they fell to the ground below. When they dusted themselves off, the face of one was dirty while the other's was clean. Only the clean-faced boy went off to wash his face. Why?

Clues

1. Neither of them needed cold water to stop bruising and neither child was hurt.
2. Neither child put their dirty hands on their faces.
3. It was dusty and they had both sweated.
4. Their faces had not touched the ground.

See answer 52

The Holiday Disaster

Bill Drallam and his lifelong companion did not like the cold weather and often flew to the warmer southern states for a winter break. This year they decided that they would go with other friends in a larger group. They reached the airport and most of the group were killed, together with 30 people they had never met before. The survivors who suffered injury who were in their group were not taken to hospital, yet all of the other survivors with injuries were. Can you explain what occurred?

Clues

1. Members from their group caused the problem.
2. They did not cause the problem deliberately.
3. No disease or virus was involved.
4. It was not a terrorist or hijack situation.
5. It had nothing to do with guns.
6. If they had not gone with the larger group the 30 strangers may have survived.

See answer 91

Evolution

Three uninhabited islands were within swimming distance from each other but only at certain times of the year. This depended on the strong currents that flowed between them. A group of naturalist explorers put animal x on island A, animal y on island B and animal z on island C. No other animals were on the islands and no animals visited the islands.

When the explorers returned several years later they found island A had no animals on it. Island B had animals x and y plus one new animal on it, and island C had the same type of animals as island B plus z and another new animal. Can you name the five animals?

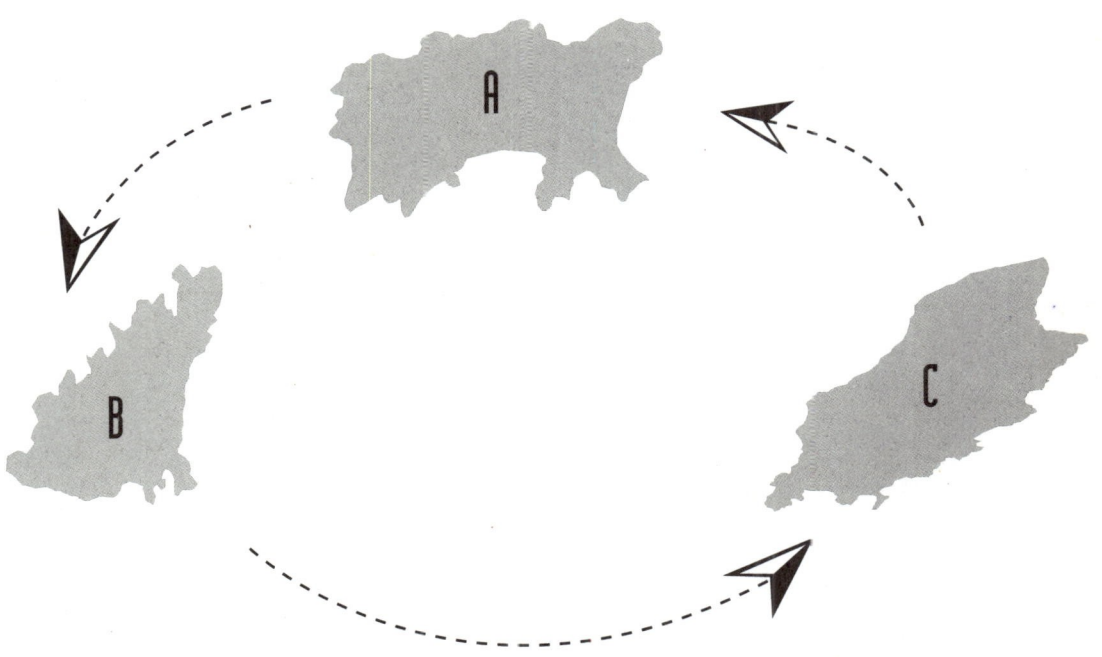

See answer 73

The Full Cask of Wine

Following a shipwreck a case of wine is washed ashore and is lodged precariously on some rocks on the seashore. The sole inhabitant of the island only has a bottle with a rubber seal which fits the bunghole at the top of the cask exactly. He also has an endless supply of fresh drinking water. He cannot move the barrel at all and cannot break the cask for fear of losing all of the contents. How does he get the wine into the bottle if he is not allowed to put water into the cask and he does not wish to spoil the wine?

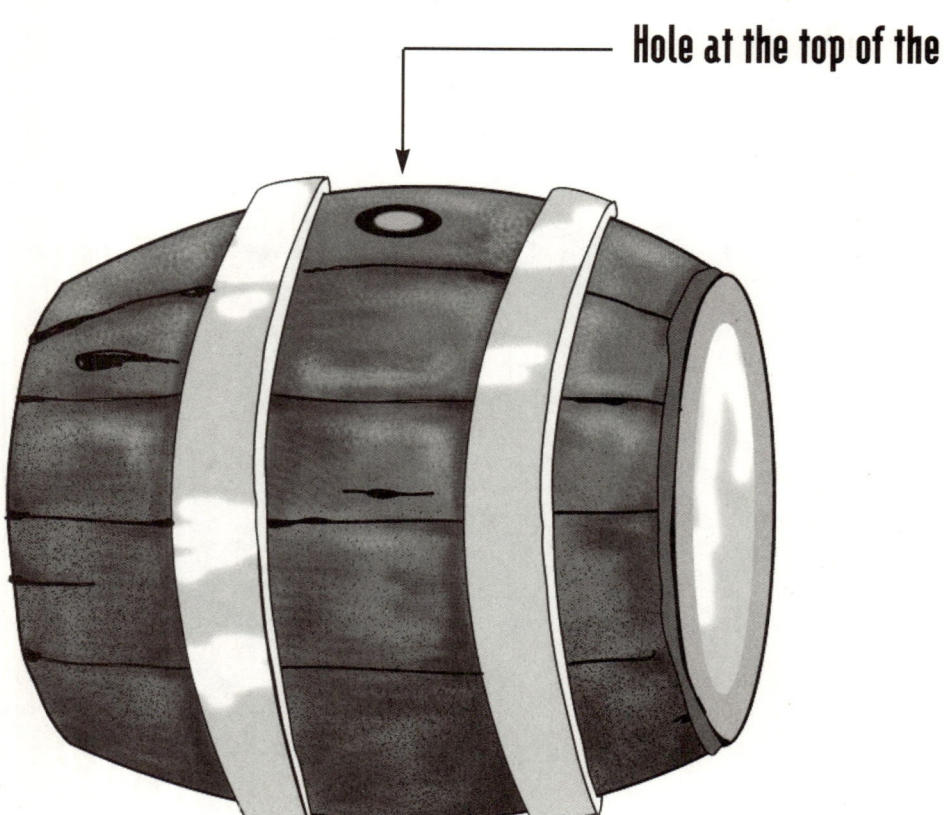

Hole at the top of the cask

See answer 100

Recovering with a Letter

A deaf lady was tricked by a conman who told her that he could make her hear if she bought a special letter from him. When she opened the envelope what did she find?

See answer 46

The Twins Cause Confusion

A father always wanted 4 sons. His ancestors had always had large families and so he thought nothing about it. He was, however, upset in later life because he had only produced 3 sons. His eldest son was now 28 years old and he had given him a quarter of his land as his inheritance already. He had not passed other shares to his other sons before a wonderful event occurred: twins, and both boys! He immediately split the remaining land into four equally shaped parts, which were also equal in area, and gave each remaining child a share. How did he do this, given that he had divided the land awkwardly?

See answer 114

How to Trick the Genie?

The king had a magic lamp that contained a genie. He also had a beautiful daughter who loved Aladdin, but the king did not like Aladdin and did not wish them to marry. He did not wish to upset his daughter, so one day he rubbed on the lamp and devised a plan with the genie. The king said he would call upon Aladdin and his daughter and seek a test of worthiness from the genie for Aladdin. They would all have to abide by the results. Aladdin was passing by when he heard the king and the genie planning the event. The genie said, "I will produce two envelopes for Aladdin to choose his fate. We will tell him that one contains the words 'Get Married' and the other will contain the words 'Banished Forever.' Aladdin must choose one envelope, but I will make sure that both envelopes have 'Banished Forever.'"

How did Aladdin trick the genie and the king?

See answer 12

Car Grid

You are in a car that is parked and facing east on a straight road. You set off in the direction of the facing road and after some time driving you finish up 2.7 miles to the west of where you started.

How?

Clues

1. It is not a car with hovering capabilities.
2. It is not on a trailer or being towed.
3. You have not gone around the world.
4. You cannot turn the car around.

See answer 81

Does It Add Up?

Two mothers and two daughters went shopping for new dresses for a wedding celebration. They each returned with a new dress, but they had only bought 3 dresses. How can this be correct?

See answer 79

Not So Scientific

What is it that you can see with the naked eye, seems to have no weight and yet the more of them you put into an empty container, the lighter the container becomes? Two answers are possible.

See answer 30

The Arctic Explorers

A man went into a seafood restaurant and ordered seal stew. After only a few mouthfuls he wrote a note to the police and then pulled out a gun and shot himself. Why?

Clues

1. He was not an unhappy man and he had not contemplated this action before going to the restaurant.
2. He chose seal stew because he had to survive on this food for 14 days on a recent expedition.
3. His note told the police that he was committing suicide and giving the reason.
4. The reason given referred to his last expedition with two friends.

See answer 15

The Gravel Quarry

Big Al and Little Joe had just robbed a jeweler's but the police were not far behind them. Their escape route went near an abandoned gravel quarry where Little Joe worked when the quarry was open. They stopped and dropped the bag containing the jewels over the edge of the rim and saw where it landed. Just to make sure it was well hidden, they threw some dry sand over the bag where it had landed. After 20 seconds they looked over the edge and they could not see the bag, and the sand blended with the damp sandy surface below. Two miles further on the police arrested the men and later had to release them for lack of evidence. Big Al killed Little Joe the next day and got away with the murder. What were the circumstances?

Clues

1. Neither of them had told the police where to find the jewels.
2. No animal, bird or person moved the jewels.
3. The jewels had gone from the spot where they were stacked.
4. Big Al did not take the jewels in the night and he did not suspect Little Joe of taking the jewels. Little Joe did not suspect Big Al of removing the jewels.
5. They remembered the correct spot exactly.
6. A warning sign had been placed so that it could not be seen from above.

See answer 60

The Silence

"Hello," said Henry, as he gave his girlfriend a peck on the cheek. He then asked, "Where's dinner?" After a few moments he said, "Your dad couldn't say that". He was right, but do you know why?

Clues
1. Her father was alive and in good health, and there was nothing wrong with his mind or voice.
2. He was born and raised in the same country as all of his offspring.
3. They still lived together and communicated every day.
4. The father was not angry with Henry.

See answer 97

Hit the Wrong Button

Adam was into all forms of sports and adventures. One day he joined an outdoor activity club, and after the necessary instructions had been given, he joined the rest of the group. The training was intense and his enthusiasm for the sport often clouded his judgment. Everything had gone well until he was on the return leg when he hit a button that caused his death. What was the sport and what button did he hit?

Clues

1. Training took a few weeks.
2. The sport required him to follow several safety rules.
3. Some people have been known to enter into the activity without training.
4. He was less than a mile from the finish when he made the mistake and was traveling at under 30 mph.

See answer 69

Little Annie

It was just after Christmas when Little Annie went to the village store to buy some candies and a few things for her mother. "That will be $10.50, Annie," said the storekeeper. Annie handed over a $10 bill and a $5 bill, and waited for her goods and change.

"I can't give you the goods or change until your mother comes in, Annie," the storekeeper explained in a very friendly tone. Why?

Clues

1. She had not purchased any tobacco, perfume, alcohol products, or anything where her age required her to be older.
2. Her mother would not have been upset with her even though she had not asked her to go to the store.
3. She often ran to the store for her mother for small items and was always partial to a few candies for her trouble.
4. She was an honest child.

See answer 102

The Magician

The magician's table is smoking with carbon dioxide gas, produced from dry ice in water. The mystery increases as he taps a smoking metal ball with his wand and places it in a wooden box, which is just big enough to enclose it. The box is placed on a tray for all to see and a few moments later the ball is gone. What was the scientific explanation for this?

Clues

1. It was a solid metal ball.
2. A small hole at the bottom of the box existed.
3. The ball was 30 times too big to go through the hole.
4. The box was hot.

See answer 14

Answers

1. Racetrack Confusion
It was his mother in car 3.

2. Uneasy Peace
The McPhersons were given the numbers :- 5, 6, 7, 8, 9, 12, 16, 18, 19, 22, 23, 24, 26, 27 & 30. If the count started at number 1 all of the McPhersons had to jump overboard.

3. Sally's Wash
The pipe to the basin has frozen so the plughole was also frozen. Therefore, as long as Sally did not run the hot tap, the water would stay in the basin.

4. Amazement
The child saw it on a TV movie.

5. The Rejected Recruit
He was trained as a sharpshooter or sniper. His type of color-blindness allowed him to pick out other snipers wearing camouflage quite easily. He was therefore a very important member of his unit since he could see the enemy and get in the first shot. [This technique has been employed especially in jungle warfare.]

6. Nylon Ball-Bearings
He fell into a storage compartment and sank to the bottom. He eventually ran out of air.

7. The Disappearing Man
He had melted; he was a snowman.

8. Head-On Ant Crash?
They asked not to go on the roc at the same time.

9. The Millionaire's Inheritance
Only if they can express the number to base 9, which gives $7,000,000 or $1,000,000 each.

10. The Policewoman
It was her husband breaking into their own house after they had locked the keys inside.

11. The Abandoned
Charlie was a cuckoo. The punctuality clue refers to a cuckoo clock.

12. How to Trick the Genie?
Aladdin chose one envelope, and without opening it, tore it up into lots of pieces, and asked the King to read what option he had rejected in the other envelope.

13. The Musical End
The music and lighting were on the same circuit. The emergency and life-support systems were on another circuit. It was night-time and when the music stopped the lights went off. In the confusion, one of the visitors accidentally disconnected some vital equipment and Grandpa died.

14. The Magician
The ball was made from frozen mercury, which melted and went through the hole in the base to a glass container. The box was left dry inside.

15. The Arctic Explorers
The three on the expedition were cut off by bad weather and had no emergency supplies. His best friend and his other colleague went for food. Only the colleague returned. For 14 days his colleague had told him that they had been eating seal stew. When he tasted seal stew in the restaurant, he realized that he had eaten his best friend.

16. Sinking Robots
The mass of the planet was much greater, although its size was the same. This meant that its gravitational forces were 10 times greater, the effect of which meant that the robots weighed 10 times what they would have done on ZOD. This caused them to sink to a level where they would not function.

17. Big Bill
Big Bill was a lighthouse keeper who had stayed awake the previous night to keep the light working in the worst part of the storm. The alarm bell on the buoy had been smashed on the rocks and no longer gave an audible warning. The lighthouse light was switched off in error and, as a result, a ship crashed on the rocks.

18. A Problem for the Ferryman
Nine trips are required. Label the children A,B,C,D, and E in ascending age, and the sides of the river "Near" and "Far" to create the table below:-

Trip No.	Near Side	Children in boat	Far Side
1.	A,C,E	B,D	None
2.	A,C,E	B	D
3.	B,E	A,C	D
4.	B,E	A,D	C
5.	B,D	A,E	C
6.	B,D	C,E	A
7.	B,D	C,E	A
8.	B,D	None	A,C,E
9.	None	B,D	A,C,E

Each child has had 3 one-way trips

19. Brother Simon
Brother Simon is a ghost and passes through the walls.

20. The Class
James is a teacher.

21. Another Mansion Murder
Abbie

22. Triangles
Ans. See image

23. The Courier's Wait
He was on a boat and had to wait for the next high tide to get into the unloading dock.

24. The Removal Men
The removal man took the stolen stamps to the biggest stamp dealer in the city, who recognized that they were stolen from his shop some years before. He called the police, who arrested both the homeowner and the removal man.

25. Hold-up Clues
The customer had hiccups. The fright of seeing the masked gunman did the same job as the water would have.

26. Little Breeders
They were all female birds.

27. The Immovable Screw
He was using a two-way screw driver, which had a clutch action. It had last been used to put a screw into a panel by turning the screw clockwise. The reversible switch to engaged the screwdriver for undoing screws had not been altered.

28. Levitating Balloons?
They had left the bath running, which overflowed through the ceiling. The draught excluders prevented the water from escaping and the water level in the room was 2 inches deep.

29. Washing Dishes
The odds of the deciding lot would be the same for each round, and over time that child (unless unlucky) would be required to wash dishes on a Sunday as many times as each of the other children.

30. Not So Scientific
Holes or beams of light

31. Mad Driver?
He saw someone cutting across from the opposite side of the road and they were spinning out of control and heading straight for him. He was boxed in, and rather than take a head-on impact, which might have killed both drivers, he took a minor bump on the car in front of him.

32. Target Practice
It had snowed overnight so they cleared the yard and made snowballs, which stuck to the barn and melted away afterwards.

33. The Burglar
The burglar had just burgled the house next door when he noticed that the neighboring house was on fire. He immediately entered the building to raise the alarm. Checking the rooms, he found two children overcome by smoke and took them to safety. The neighbors saw what had gone missing, and it was still in the burglar's hand when they called the police.

34. The Deadwood Stagecoach
He woke up (still drunk) on the stagecoach, which was still at the saloon. He needed the stagecoach to take him away.

35. The Fabric Shop
The curtains also have horizontal lines, so they are checked.

36. Antony & Cleopatra
They were both pet fish and the tank that housed them had a crack; all the water had leaked away.

37. Moving Suitcases
A violent tornado had ripped through their apartment and carried the contents over a few miles. A kind lady found the cases in her yard; because the address labels had not been filled in, she decided to place them at the side of the road so that the owner might see them if they drove past. Because of the damage a few miles away, the police were keen to help the homeless and rescue services. That was the reason for not passing the property on to the police.

38. High Days and Holidays
Saturday, Wednesday, Thursday, Tuesday, Sunday, Monday & Friday (sum of alphabetical positions)

39. Disappearing Treat
The bag contained candyfloss. Rain got into the hole in the top of the bag, and the candy dissolved into a small amount of pink liquid.

40. A-Haunting We Will Go!
Take the room number at present multiplied by the number of days between the sightings, and then subtract the number of days between sightings. The number of days between sightings increases by one for each period. The next sighting will be $(9 \times 4) - 4 = 32$, thus Room 32 every fifth night.

41. Amateur Safe-crackers
Like the expression from the firing

of flintlock rifles "a flash in the pan," they had not compacted the powder or kept it in a container to cause an explosion. It therefore ignited like the powder in the "pan" of a flintlock rifle and just went up in a flash and a great cloud of smoke. In olden times the "charge" of powder was compacted inside the barrel of the rifle. A small charge of loose powder was placed in a small bowl where the flint's spark would ignite the powder in the pan, which then lit the compressed powder in the barrel through a small hole. Once ignited, the compacted powder would cause the bang and the shot to be fired.

42. Survival of the Weakest?

Your first shot should go behind you or deliberately in the air. You can't shoot at Count Nevermiss because if you did and were unlucky enough to hit him, Lord Bullseye would polish you off with the next shot or two. If you shoot at Lord Bullseye and hit, Count Nevermiss will certainly get you. If you miss Lord Bullseye, Count Nevermiss would not and his chances against you are 2 : 1 in his favour. If you hit Count Nevermiss, Lord Bullseye's probability of winning against you is 6/7, yours is 1/7. But if you deliberately miss, you will have another shot against either one of the other two. If Lord Bullseye hits the Count, you will have a 3/7 probability. With 1/2 probability, the Lord will miss the Count (in which case the Count will dispose of the Lord). Thus your chance's are 1/3 against the Count. The odds are increased by shooting in the air: the first shot will be 25/63 (about 40%) Lord Bullseye's odds become 8/21 (38%); Count Nevermiss's odds are 2/9 (22%).

43. The Fire

They were explorers who had built an igloo. The fire was too big and melted the walls when they fell asleep. They both suffered extreme hypothermia and died.

44. Happy New Year and Again and Again etc.

She was an astronaut, who on one occasion was in a stationary orbit over the Greenwich Date Line. As each date line revolved below her, she celebrated the New Year 24 times. The other times occurred while she flew from east to west, passing through three date lines when it was midnight on the ground.

45. The Strong Swimmer

A break in the seabed released large quantities of trapped air as small bubbles. This reduced the density of the water so that it was lower than the density of a human body and he sank.

46. Recovering with a Letter

A piece of paper with the letter 'A' on it. The instructions said, "If you add 'A' to 'her,' you will have 'hear.'"

47. The Casino

They were a band who played background music for the guests. They were paid by the casino and did not gamble.

48. Charged by a Bull

One of the family named BULL who owns the nearby farm charged them $20 to cross his land.

49. Don't Jump to Conclusions

He was a priest whose birth had been in the presence of his father.

50. Leap to Safety

His house is built into a hill/ the house is built below ground level.

51. The Aircraft

It was the earliest days of commercial jet aircraft flight and a few unexplained accidents involving the Comet needed to be investigated. The Comet was the first commercial transatlantic passenger jet. It flew higher and faster than all other commercial planes, and was therefore subjected to stresses that other planes had not endured. The main problems came when the pressures in the fusilage were greater than those outside. The design engineers found that this was best simulated by putting water in the fusilage under pressure. This identified a number of weaknesses in the design, especially around the windows. The findings have made all jet travel much safer.

52. In the Dirt

One child fell on his feet, and his face was not covered with dust to make his face dirty. When he saw his friend's face covered in dust, he thought his own must also be dirty; his friend only saw his friend's clean face. The dirty child did not think that he needed to wash.

53. The Savage Attack

The lady was in a shopping mall and suffered a heart attack. Her heart had just stopped. The man who came to the woman's aid was a doctor just passing by. He started her heart, put her into his car, and drove straight to a nearby hospital with a police escort. The police were initially a little slow, and had to pursue him before clearing a way for him.

54. Who Is The Bigger Liar?
It was prisoner D. He lied twice but nobody said that he did not leave the cell for a few minutes to steal the sugar.

55. Trackside Jo
His bet was for a race two weeks earlier when the horse trailed in last. The newspaper gave the previous day's results when the horse had won.

56. The Tea Party
The little girl was in her playhouse. She had to go through the front door of the playhouse first, and then the front door of the family house to get to the front garden.

57. 1930s
It was a seaplane. The water that it was to use at the first landing sight was too rough for a safe landing so the pilot diverted to an airfield on land.

58. The Master Forger
They wanted to substitute the $50 note in his flat with a $50 note with a flaw in it. This flaw was unique to that note only, and when more of them hit the streets it could be traced back to him alone.

59. The Jealous Husbands
Men = ABC   Women = abc

Near Bank	Boat	Opposite Bank
ACac	**Bb**	**None**
Acac	B	b
ABC	ac	b
ABC	a	bc
Aa	BC	bc
Aa	Bb	Cc
ab	AB	Cc
ab	c	ABC
b	ac	ABC
b	B	Acac
None	Bb	Acac

60. The Gravel Quarry
The jewels were thrown on to quicksand. Little Joe had forgotten about it, but Big Al made him try to get the jewels. Little Joe tried and sank without trace. The police did not even know that Little Joe was dead.

61. Cardinal Lock'emup
One of the inkwells had disappearing ink. When the Captain of Guards saw nothing except the seals, he arrested the musketeers until he could speak to the Cardinal.

62. The Cup of Coffee
He had put sugar in the first cup.

63. The Messy Eater
He brings tinned fruit or pre-prepared fruit.

64. The Arabian Prince's Car
The clear plastic sucker that attached the air freshener to the front windscreen was shaped like a lens and focused the sun's rays like a magnifying glass on to the newspaper. The paper caught fire, causing the damage.

65. Lost for Days
Sunday

66. The Puzzle King of Eygpt
The cube has two diagonal dovetail slots. The top can be pushed off by pushing at 45º to the face.

67. Lottery Winners
$230,000 ($15,000 increments)

68. Arise
It was an undersea mountain, and natural buoyancy lifted him.

69. Hit the Wrong Button
It was a parachute jump. He had hit the release button after his shoot had been deployed.

70. The Great Soccer Player Retires
He played the whole of the first half, and for 10 minutes of the second half for his club. He scored 2 goals for his club in the first half. He was then taken off the field of play, and invited to play for his country for the last 35 minutes, scoring twice more. The other deciding goal was an "own goal" not scored by him.

71. A Bargain
The land was being reclaimed from the sea for industrial use. His company owned the reclamation contract. The land would soon be worth a fortune.

72. Father vs Son
Joe beat him at a game of chess (or something similar).

73. Evolution
Animal X on island A was an ass. Animal Y on island B was a horse. Animal Z on island C was a donkey. The new animal on island B was a MULE (ass/mare). The new animal on island C was a HINNEY (Donkey/Stallion).

74. The Last Train
His watch had 3 hands. The hour hand was obscured by the minute hand. This occurs every 65.4545 minutes after 12 o'clock.

75. The Bus Drivers
The two bus drivers are married; one is the boy's mother and the other is the his father.

76. King-Elect
Only the less-bright child was a male.

77. The Bath of Liquid
He fell into a storage bath containing mercury. He was taken to hospital to be decontaminated because mercury can cause health problems. At room temperature mercury does not leave the skin feeling wet.

78. Confusion & Lies
If you say the child was a boy then the second speaker must have been the mother, whose first statement must have been a lie and whose second statement was true. But boys in the family do not lie so this option is no good. If you say that the child was a girl and if the first speaker was the father, then the second speaker was the mother whose first statement would be true and whose second statement was a lie. In that case the child would have spoken the truth and would have said, "I am a girl". But this implies that the first speaker lied, but males cannot lie. This option is therefore no good. So by deduction the first speaker was the mother and the child said, "I am a boy." The first statement from both the mother and child were lies. The child was a girl.

79. Does it Add Up?
They were grandmother, mother, and daughter. Two were mothers and two were daughters.

80. Alien Conference
107

81. Car Grid
After going forward, you reverse.

82. The King Is In His All-Together!
It was a birthday parade where all of the participants carried pictures of themselves at birth.

83. Bush Fire
To put out the fire they used airplanes to scoop water out of the nearest lake. When they scooped the water out, they scooped him out as well. Water dropped on the fire and put it out but the fall killed the diver.

84. Household Enquiry
"Sally, are you in?" or "Are you there?" etc.

85. A Fruity Problem
The fruits are made of wax; they are candles, and the woman lit them before leaving the room so that they had burned down.

86. The Cheetah & the Hyena
Thursday

87. Golfers
They were playing darts in the clubhouse. The object of the challenge was to see who could score the most with just 3 darts.

88. St. Joseph's Church
His father was the Italian Ambassador and he moved from Rome to Washington. Daniel only spoke Italian.

89. A Body Bag in the Suitcase
He was a part-time ventriloquist and it was his dummy.

90. My Homework is Right!
He was adding hours to his watch. 10 o'clock + 7 hrs = 5 o'clock.

91. The Holiday Disaster
Bill Drallam (Mallard backwards) was a duck. They flew in front of a plane during lift-off and entered the engine intake, causing the plane to crash. The plane might have survived if only one or two ducks flew into the engine, but several birds were hit and drawn into other engines.

92. Leaky Pipe
The second leak was halfway up the pipe. The first half was emptied in 1 hour, and with just the single leak left for the water to exit, it took another two hours.

93. The Inherited House
The sea had eroded the cliffs to within 30 yards of the garden. He found that it would be uneconomical to protect the house from further erosion. Experts had told him that it might only be 5 years before the mansion would be in the sea.

94. Cheap Shopper!
He had replaced all of the bar codes on the products with labels taken off small packs of the same items. The products he bought were all large packs and the bill should have been at least 3 times more. The shop assistant at the till raised the alarm when she saw one of the bar code labels was loose.

95. Two Brothers
The letter contained a white feather, a symbol of cowardice. In order to rid his family name of this slur, he was forced to act with bravery.

96. Dangerous Neighbors?
Mark. The policeman interpreted the question as "Question Mark Price!"

97. The Silence
Henry was the only parrot in the cage that could talk.

98. No Fire for Explorers
Neil and Dave were astronauts conducting an experiment on the Moon.

The lack of oxygen caused all of their problems.

99. The Meeting
Rain, for which Iran is an anagram (as Nepal is an anagram for plane, and China for chain).

100. The Full Cask of Wine
He washes some small pebbles and sand with the fresh water, and puts the washed and dried materials into the bottle. He then puts the bottleneck into the bunghole. The pebbles and sand will fill into the cask to be replaced by wine into the bottle.

101. Problems With Air Pollution
Nobody lived to the east of the chemical plant.

102. Little Annie
Annie had been given a Monopoly game for Christmas and used money from its bank to purchase the goods. The storekeeper was not offended as he knew her very well.

103. The Share-Out
Child 1 had 10 25¢ coins, Child 2 had 16 10¢ coins, and Child 3 had 26 5¢ coins.

104. The Awkward Piano
The items stacked on the piano had fallen toward Joe, and he had said to Alf, "Give me a hand to move them off!" Alf rushed into the department store and removed a hand from a mannequin and put it in Joe's top pocket.

105. The Unlucky Locksmith
The locksmith had been shut in with the manager after he had set the automatically activated system. He was inside the room just collecting the last items from the manager. The room had no light and the lock could not be tampered with from the inside.

106. The Fan
While he was celebrating it rained. The blue paint he had put on first was insoluble, but the yellow he put on top to create green was soluble, and had all washed off.

107. The Fire Drill
A swarm of killer bees had been sighted just outside the school.

108. The Hotel Fire
It was bonfire night (5th November) and the clothes from the dummy (called the "guy") were burning.

109. Car Park Overcrowding
Make all of the car park spaces at right angles to the wall.

110. Bob the Miser's Last Will
The Judge ruled that the money be shared equally between the relatives, but that they should each give Bob a money order for the money taken. If these were not cashed within 1 year of Bob's cremation, then the money could be kept.

111. Lateral Thinking Gem From Times gone by
10TO10 (Ten to Ten or 9.50 time)

112. Corporal in the Army
He was in uniform.

113. Is the Doctor Wrong?
It was the consultant physician supervising the student doctor who suffered the cardiac arrest. The student's prompt action saved his life. The farmworker was checked out, given a temporary plaster casing on his ankle, and was later allowed to go home.

114. The Twins Cause Confusion

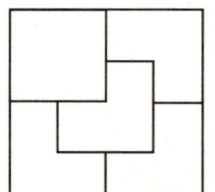

115. The Glass Head
The two parts were lined up using strings with weights to guide the head down. Several piles of sugar or other water-soluble materials were stacked at strategic locations on the plinth. The head was lowered and the ropes removed. The piles were then treated with a water spray starting from the central piles. (Dry ice could also be used.)

116. The Mountaineers
They were travelling to their destination by cruise ship. The hull of the ship was rammed during the night, and their cabin was below the water line. The pressure of the water held the door shut, they could not escape, and the rescuers were too late to save them.